The 101 Coolest Things to Do in Scotland

Introduction

So you're going to Scotland, huh? You lucky lucky thing! You are sure in for a treat because Scotland is truly one of the most magical countries on this planet. There's a mix of incredible religious and historic architecture, a culinary scene that is growing in strength every day, thrilling outdoor activities, and nightlife and parties that makes Scotland one of the most enduringly popular tourist destinations on the planet.

In this guide, we'll be giving you the low down on:
- the very best things to shove in your pie hole, from hearty classics like haggis to dishes in Michelin star restaurants
- incredible adventure activities, from deep sea diving through to surfing lessons
- the best shopping so that you can take a little piece of Scotland back home with you, whether that's in the form of Shetland sweater or something from a flea market
- the coolest historical and cultural sights that you simply cannot afford to miss, from the medieval ruins to stunning cathedrals
- amazing festivals from beer festivals to outdoor music gatherings

- where to party like a local person and make Scottish friends
- and tonnes more coolness besides!

Let's not waste any more time – here are the 101 coolest things not to miss in Scotland!

1. Feel the Fun of the Edinburgh Fringe Festival

Every August, the population of Edinburgh doubles. Why? The Edinburgh Fringe Festival. This is the largest Fringe festival to be found anywhere in the world, and it's the perfect place to catch an up and coming show, whether you're into stand-up, musicals, or physical theatre. At the same time as the Fringe Fest, there's also a film festival and a television festival, so this is 100% the place to be if you're interested in the arts. August also comes to life with lots of all-night parties at the various Fringe venues across the city. *(www.edfringe.com)*

2. Gobble Up Haggis, Neeps, and Tatties

Okay, Scotland might not exactly be the culinary capital of Europe, but this is not to say that there are no delights to sample, and if there is one local food that you can't leave without trying, it's the famous (or should that be infamous?) haggis. Haggis is a savoury dish that comprises the heart, liver, and lungs of a sheep. These are mixed together with suet, oats, and spice, and boiled in the stomach of an animal, which it is usually served in. Errr.... delicious? And don't forget the neeps and tatties – these are the potatoes and turnips served alongside haggis.

3. Take a Beautiful Walk Along the Sandwood Bay

When setting off on a trip to Scotland, you probably don't imagine yourself having beach days, but you might be surprised by just how stunning the beaches in Scotland are, and Sandwood Bay has even been named the most beautiful beach in Britain. If you like your beaches wild and unspoiled, Sandwood is 100% for you. You'll find 1.5 miles of wild pink sand, dramatic cliffs, and beyond the cliffs you can find undulating sand dunes.

4. Down a Few at the Ayrshire Real Ale Festival

The Scots are serious about their love of beer, and never is this more evident than at the Ayrshire Real Ale Festival, which is held every October over a long weekend in the Troon Concert Hall. As you walk through the aisles, you will be presented with a staggering selection of more than 150 ales, all of which are produced in the UK. There are also tutored tastings, as well as live music in the evenings. *(www.ayrshirebeerfestival.co.uk)*

5. Have a Whale Watching Adventure

Did you know that the west coast of Scotland is one of the very best places for whale watching adventures in the world? The North Minch, a strait in north-west Scotland, is particularly rich in marine life, and it's here that you can find a number of whale watching opportunities through tour companies who will take you out on a boat and make sure that you are really close to all of the action. You might also sea dolphins, porpoises, sharks, seals, and otters.

6. Feel the Creativity of Glasgow at Urban Market

To get a sense of the incredible creativity that exists within Scotland, you have to visit the Urban Market in Glasgow. It takes place on the first and third Sunday of the month at the Drygate Brewing Co, and it's a place where the traders are selected very carefully. You'll find a wonderful selection of people committed to their craft, whether that's creating original leather goods, innovative ceramics, or hand crafted jewellery. There is also delicious food and craft beers available to purchase.

(85 Drygate, Glasgow; http://drygate.com/events/urban-market-(1))

7. Sip on a Flying Scotsman Cocktail

Those Scots sure do love to booze, but if you aren't so keen on drinking your Scotch straight, there are plenty of ways that you can get a hit of Scotch inside a cocktail. One of the enduring favourites is the Flying Scotsman, named after a train that took passengers from London to Edinburgh and back again in the 19th century. This glass of deliciousness is a mix of Scotch whisky, Italian vermouth, bitters, and just a little cane sugar. Needless to say, two of these and you'll be feeling merry as a Scot – the perfect thing for a lazy Sunday evening at the hotel before a week of epic sightseeing.

8. Climb Arthur's Seat for a View to Die For

You'll need some strong lungs for this one, but if you love the outdoors, this is guaranteed to be the highlight of your trip to bonny Scotland. Arthur's Seat is the main peak in Holyrood Park, a park that can be found on the outskirts of Edinburgh. It's 251 metres above sea level, allowing you to experience *the* most breath taking view of Edinburgh that can be found. It's only a 45 minute walk from the park so it makes from a memorable morning excursion that's accessible to anyone with moderate fitness.

9. Get Decadent With Afternoon Tea at The Balmoral

When you visit a new city or a new country for the first time, it's important to be a little bit indulgent, and there is nothing more British nor more indulgent than a classic afternoon tea at The Balmoral in Edinburgh. Their afternoon tea is served in a beautiful champagne bar with a glass dome and palm trees inside. You can expect all the classics such as scones with clotted cream, finger sandwiches, and, of course, pots and pots of tea.

(The Balmoral, 1 Princes St, Edinburgh)

10. Embrace Your Inner Infant at the Museum of Childhood

Whether you are travelling with kids or you just so happen to be a big kid yourself, the Museum of Childhood in Edinburgh makes for a playful afternoon well spent. This museum was actually the first ever to specialise in the history of childhood, and you and your kids will be able to explore all kinds of toys and games from the decades and centuries gone past. Check out their programme of events because they often have exciting workshops in their schedule.

(42 High St, Royal Mile, Edinburgh;
www.edinburghmuseums.org.uk/Venues/Museum-of-Childhood)

11. Go Cycling in the Pentland Hills

If you are spending some time in Edinburgh but you would rather escape the capital city for a day and breathe in some fresh Scottish air, you can't do much better than the nearby Pentland Hills, which extend for around 20 miles, just southwest of Edinburgh. These hills are extremely popular with cyclists and there are various routes to suit all kinds of cycling abilities.

12. Chow Down on a Traditional Scotch Egg

Although Scotland may not have an international reputation for its food, this does not mean that there are not plenty of delicious treats to chow down on, and there is no better summer picnic treat than a traditional Scotch egg. If you've not sampled one of these before, it is a hard boiled egg that is wrapped in sausage meat, covered in breadcrumbs, and then fried. You'll find them in many of the traditional pubs around the country.

13. Visit an Aberdeen Angus Farm

If you are a lover of steak, you have no doubt heard of Aberdeen Angus beef already, which is known the world over for its rich flavour. Well, on your trip to Scotland, you can actually visit a farm that specialises in Aberdeen Angus cows, and that's Wynford Farm. The farm is very family friendly with a PlayBarn area where you can leave small children, while you eat something delicious in the farm café. And, of course, you can take back some steaks from the farm shop too.

(Kingswells, Aberdeen; www.wynfordfarm.com)

14. Get Back to Nature at the Royal Botanic Garden Edinburgh

Edinburgh is not the kind of capital city that is full of hustle and bustle, but if you still feel as though you need to escape city life for a morning, it's a great idea to pass some time in the Royal Botanic Garden Edinburgh. Amazingly, the gardens date way back to the 17th century, and today they contain more than 13,000 plant species. There are many different gardens to explore, from a Scottish heath garden through to a Chinese hillside.

(Arboretum Pl, Edinburgh; www.rbge.org.uk)

15. Explore Art and Culture at the Junkyard Festival

If you happen to be in Glasgow during the summer months, we can guarantee that making it to Junkyard Festival will be your summer highlight. Junkyard Festival is really unique because it's an urban celebration of everything in Glasgow – culture, art, food, drink, and music. It takes place at the end of July, and visitors have the chance to sip on craft beers while listening to experimental bands, and taking home something special from Glasgow based designers.

16. Eat a Decadent Meal at The Gardener's Cottage

There are so many restaurants in Edinburgh that it can be hard to know which ones to pick for the most memorable meals if you are only there for a short time. Well, a restaurant that has never disappointed us and is popular with critics and diners alike is The Gardener's Cottage. The restaurant really is located in the ex-cottage of a gardener, and dates back to 1836. It's beautiful and the food is even better. If the hake is on the menu, be sure to order it.

(294 Colinton Rd, Edinburgh; www.thegardenerscottage.co)

17. Take a Stroll on Cramond Island

When you're in Edinburgh and you feel as though you need to escape the city, one very easy day trip that you can make is to Cramond Island. Cramond Island is a tidal island that only exists 1.6km out to sea, and you don't even need a boat to get there. At low tide, a path is exposed that you can walk across to get to the island. The island is very simple and peaceful, and that's the whole beauty of it – just make sure you don't get stuck there at high tide!

18. Take a Quiet Walk Along the Water of Leith

Like any great city, Edinburgh has a river running through it – the river Leith. This river starts in the Pentland Hills and flows downwards through the city, and when the river reaches Edinburgh, there is a river walkway alongside the water that makes it perfect for a peaceful afternoon stroll. On your way, you will see Murrayfield Stadium, the Scottish National Gallery of Modern Art, the Royal Botanic Garden, and many other treasures of the city.

19. Have an Artsy Day at the Scottish National Gallery of Modern Art

While the art galleries of London might be better known, do not discount Edinburgh as an arts city, as it is incredibly committed to all facets of the arts, including the visual arts. For contemporary art, the most impressive place is the Scottish National Gallery of Modern Art. There you will find a collection of more than 6000 drawings, paintings, sculptures, photographs, and video work, including works by Barbara Hepworth, Salvador Dali, and Martin Creed. *(75 Belford Rd, Edinburgh; www.nationalgalleries.org)*

20. Down Some Pints at Jocktoberfest

Love beers? Love a good party? Of course you do! And that's why you need to know about Jocktoberfest, the greatest Scottish beer festival of them all. The festival is run annually by the Black Isle Brewery, and it takes place every September just outside of Inverness. The festival is hosted outdoors, and each year there are live bands playing as well as great beers to drink. If you want to have the real festival experience, you can camp out too.

21. Indulge in Fish Pie at The Witchery

If you want to have a meal that you remember forever in Scotland, make sure that you reserve a table at The Witchery

in Edinburgh. The restaurant really does occupy a magical space with medieval furnishings, tapestries on the wall, and a real old world feel that transports you back in time. What's more, the food is also fantastic and we are particularly fanatical about the fish pie, which is heaving with locally caught fish and seafood. Just be sure to book a table in advance.
(Castlehill, The Royal Mile, Edinburgh; http://thewitchery.com)

22. Experience a Scottish Ceilidh at Ghillie Dhu

In Scottish Folklore, the Ghillie Dhu is the name for a male fairy, but say the word on the streets of Edinburgh and everyone will point you to the venue of the same name. Ghillie Dhu is the number one place to have a truly Scottish night out on the town. While you can eat dinner there, it is best known for its traditional ceilidhs, which essentially a knees up with folk music, traditional dancing, and storytelling. (2 Rutland St, Edinburgh; http://ghillie-dhu.co.uk)

23. Tuck Into a Traditional Scottish Dessert

While Scotland might be better known for hearty stews and meat dishes like haggis, the country does have a handful of delicious desserts hidden up its sleeve. If you like creamy, fruity desserts, you are likely to fall head over heels for cranachan, which can be thought of as Scotland's answer to trifle. It is made with toasted oatmeal that is soaked in whisky, raspberries, cream, and honey. It's pretty much the perfect way to end any meal.

24. Check out the Penguin Parade at Edinburgh Zoo

Question: Is there anything cuter than a waddling penguin? Answer: No. And as luck would have it, you can catch a whole parade of Penguins every single afternoon at 2:15pm at the world famous Edinburgh Zoo. If you think that this sounds a little exploitative, rest assured that no penguin is forced to take part in the parade and they all decide themselves if they want to strut their stuff each afternoon. *(134 b Corstorphine Rd, Edinburgh; www.edinburghzoo.org.uk)*

25. Chow Down on Dairy at The Cheese Pantry

If you are a cheese lover, your decision to visit Scotland was a very good one indeed, because this country is a cheese paradise. The Cheese Pantry is a cheese shop and café that is located slap bang within an actual dairy in the Inverness area, so you can be sure that you will be munching on the real deal. We recommend arriving on an empty stomach and ordering the full cheese board so you can try a whole breadth of Scottish cheeses.

(Connage Highland Dairy, Milton of Connage, Ardersier)

26. Eat Some Deliciousness at Stockbridge Market

When you are in Edinburgh, make sure that you don't confine yourself to the city centre, because there is always tonnes of stuff going on in the suburbs, and we are particularly partial to Stockbridge Market, which takes place every Sunday. We think it's the most wonderful place to have an alfresco breakfast on a crisp Edinburgh morning, and because it's located on the water's edge, you'll also have a spectacular view with your morning pastry and coffee.

(1 Saunders St, Edinburgh; www.stockbridgemarket.com)

27. Visit the Stunning Steall Waterfall

What could possibly be more relaxing than sitting in front of a waterfall and watching the water cascade down? Well, there are plenty of waterfalls to be enjoyed in Scotland, and perhaps the most impressive of them all is Steal Waterfall. This waterfall is actually the second highest in the country, and its sharp drop of 120 metres is breath taking to say the least. Fortunately, it's very easy to walk to, so why not pack up a picnic and enjoy the view?

28. Eat the Best Lobster of Your Life in Crail

When you think of a slap up lobster dinner, you might associate it more strongly with Mediterranean cuisine, but the nutritious waters of the Scottish seas actually produce really delicious and plump lobsters. The coast of Crail is particularly well known for the tastiness of its lobsters, and if you want the best lobster dinner of your life, waste no time and make your reservation at The Lobster Hut. The name isn't an attempt to be cute, the restaurant really is a wooden hut, but don't let that put you off – the lobster is divine.

29. Visit a Weekend Market in Glasgow

If you are something of a shopaholic and find yourself in Glasgow, bypass the high street stores, and instead save your pennies for the exceptional Barras Market, which takes place every weekend. The word "barra" is a dialectical form of the word wheelbarrow, because originally the traders used to sell their wares from handcarts. The building opened in the 1930s, and since then the market has been going strong, and you can find anything from jewellery to clothes, and antiques to paintings.

(Gallowgate, Townhead, Glasgow; www.theglasgowbarras.com)

30. Take a Turkish Bath in Portobello Swim Centre

When you think of Scotland, Turkish Baths probably aren't the first thing to come to mind, but if it's Turkish Baths you will want, it's Turkish Baths you shall have, and the baths at the Portobello Swim Centre are something very unique in Edinburgh. After a long day of sightseeing and hopping from the museum to museum, the hot baths, steam rooms, and plunge pools will be just the ticket for a relaxing and blissful experience.

(57 Promenade, Edinburgh)

31. Eat Incredible Fish & Chips in Anstruther

What could be more British, or more delicious, than a plate of fish and chips? While in Scotland, you'll find numerous fish and chips shops, but for the very best, you can't beat a trip to the small coastal town of Anstruther. Over the years, the Anstruther Fish Bar has won numerous awards and accolades, and attracted celebrities and even royalty through its doors. There is an also an ice cream parlour on-site, so dessert is sorted as well.

(42 - 44 Shore St, Anstruther; www.anstrutherfishbar.co.uk)

32. Feel Scotland's History at the Celtic & Pictish Festival

History buffs will have a ball in Scotland, but if you prefer learning things through immersion rather than walking along the corridors of museums, you will have a great time at the annual Celtic & Pictish Festival. The Celts lived in Scotland from the 5th to the 1st centuries BC, and the Picts lived in the country in the early medieval period. This festival is a wonderful way of learning about these groups, with re-enactments, archaeological digs, demos in carving, and lots more fun.

33. Enjoy a Game of Golf in St Andrews

If your idea of a perfect getaway is packing up your golf clubs and hitting a few balls, Scotland is the perfect holiday destination for you. While there are courses all over the country, the most renowned area for golf is St Andrews. There are seven golf courses in and around the city, but the most famous is certainly the Old Course. This course is actually one of the oldest in the world as it opened in 1552, and it was the first course where the standard 18 holes was created.

(The Links House, W Sands Rd, St Andrews; www.standrews.com/Play/Courses/Old-course)

34. Nibble on Dunsyre Blue Cheese

The UK is a nation full of cheese lovers, and you'll find some of the strongest and most delicious cheese up in Scotland. One that we're particularly fond of is Dunsyre Blue, which is made from the unpasteurised milk of Ayrshire cows, and it is then mould ripened to give it a blue vein and a very strong flavour. Head up to Lanarkshire in Scotland where it is produced to sample the very best of it.

35. Go Fishing on Loch Arkaig

Scotland is a country with many rivers and lakes, which makes it a spectacular destination for fishing enthusiasts. If nothing makes you happier than a peaceful afternoon of fly fishing, we think that Loch Arkaig can't be beaten. The fishing season runs from March to October when you can find plentiful supplies of wild brown trout, ferox trout, and large specimen pike – all perfect for a delicious fish supper.

36. Look for Otters at the Falls of Clyde

Scotland is the place to go for nature lovers, and if you can't get enough of waterfalls, you need to visit the Falls of Clyde, which is actually a natural complex of four different falls. The area is beautiful if you simply want to hike and take in the vistas, but what makes the place extra special is the wildlife here. This is the best place in Scotland to spot European otters in their natural habitat.

(New Lanark Road, New Lanark; http://scottishwildlifetrust.org.uk/visit/visitor-centres/falls-of-clyde)

37. Battered Mars Bar Anyone?

If you're not a Brit, you may not be accustomed to the culinary delight of the Mars Bar. This sweet treat is a combination of milk chocolate, soft nougat, and caramel. You can buy one of these treats in any cornershop across the UK, but those bonny Scots take the humble Mars Bar to the next level by immersing it in batter and hot fat. That's right – you'll be able to find deep fried mars bars in the fish and chip shops of Scotland, particularly in Glasgow. You can't leave before trying one.

38. Go Windsurfing off the Isle of Tiree

Tiree is an island in the Hebrides that is not often visited by tourists, but if you can't get enough of adrenaline pumping adventures, you should definitely put it on your must-visit list. The island has a population of 650 people, and against all odds, it's the windsurfing capital of Britain. If you are a total beginner, there is a windsurf school that can give you lessons, and if you are more advanced, you might want to visit for the professional windsurfing competition that is hosted there annually.

(www.isleoftiree.com)

39. Sample a Malt at the Arran Distillery

It is no secret that Scotland is a nation of whisky lovers and that a great deal of great quality whisky is produced in the country. If you want to take your whisky appreciation to the next level, it can be a great idea to get to grips with the whisky making process at a distillery, and one of our favourites is the Arran Distillery on the Isle of Arran. The island has a long history of producing single malt whisky but had done so illegally until this distillery opened in 1995. *(www.arranwhisky.com)*

40. Take Surfing Lessons at Thurso

Where are the best destinations in the world? You might immediately think of Hawaii or the Pacific coast of Mexico, but there is also some pretty good surfing in Scotland. Thurso, which happens to be the northernmost town on the British mainland, attracts surfers from all over the world. There are surf schools in the town, so if you feel like braving the waves, you can rent some equipment, take some lessons, and show the chilly waters of Scotland what you've got.

41. Visit the 14th Century Castle Linked to Macbeth

If historic architecture is what does it for you, you will have plenty to explore during your time in Scotland, and we think that one of the most special castles has to be Cawdor Castle. The castle is not only a beautiful piece of Scottish architecture, but it will resonate with bibliophiles as it has a connection with Shakespeare's Macbeth. In the play, Macbeth is made the Thane of Cawdor. The castle also has beautiful gardens, some of which date back to the 17th century.

(www.cawdorcastle.com/Home.aspx)

42. Eat the Best Burger of Your Life

You probably haven't trekked all the way to Scotland to chow down on burgers, but let's face it, there are times when only a juicy burger between soft bread buns will hit the spot. For our money, the best burger to be found in all of Scotland can be located at The Huxley in Edinburgh. We love it because it doesn't mess around. It's a classic burger – meat, cheese, and bread, and we wouldn't have it any other way. If you want to make the burger a little more Scottish, the staff will be happy to oblige by placing some crispy fried haggis in your bun as well.

(1-3 Rutland St, Edinburgh; www.thehuxley.co.uk)

43. Watch Movies at the Edinburgh International Film Festival

Yes, walking around all the museums and historic attractions is fantastic, but sometimes all you want to do is kick back with a good movie, right? Well, you'll have ample opportunity to do exactly that if you coincide your trip with the Edinburgh International Film Festival, which takes place each year in June. This is actually the world's oldest continuous film festival, and so it's a must visit for true cinema fans who want to catch something extra special before it hits the public. *(www.edfilmfest.org.uk)*

44. Visit a Castle on the Edge of Loch Ness

Most people around the world have heard of Loch Ness because of the mythical creature that some people believe exists in the lake. Although it's a fun story, it can overshadow the very real and very impressive castle that exists on the edge of the lake. Urquhart Castle is a medieval site dating back to the 13th century, and it's a place where you can feel the incredible history of Scotland while also taking in beautiful vistas of Loch Ness.

(Drumnadrochit, Inverness; www.urquhart-castle.co.uk)

45. Embrace Folk Music at Shetland Folk Festival

The UK is a nation with all kinds of different cultures, and if you would like to explore the folk traditions and folk music of Scotland in centuries gone by, be sure to book your ticket for the Shetland Folk Festival, which takes place every year at the end of April. You'll find everything from local fiddle players to incredible Scottish dancers, and, of course, parties that continue well into the early hours of the morning.

(www.shetlandfolkfestival.com)

46. Go Mountain Biking at Laggan Wolftrax

Fancy yourself as something of an adventurer? If so, you might find that the landscapes of Scotland were created with the sole intention of indulging your adventurous spirit. Make your way to the Laggan Forest and you will find something special called the Laggan Wolftrax Centre, which has created a network of bike trails through the forest for mountain bikers of various abilities. If you want to explore the Scottish landscape in a thrilling way, this is a must.

(http://scotland.forestry.gov.uk/visit/laggan-wolftrax)

47. Party in the Grounds of a 13th Century Castle

If you're a party person, yes you'll enjoy the nightclubs of Edinburgh and Glasgow, but you should also take the time to explore the country's various summer festivals. Kelburn Garden Party might just be the best kept secret on Europe's festival circuit. Yes, there is banging music, performances, and people out to have a good time, but what makes it really special is that the festival is set on the grounds of a 13th century painted castle, Kelburn Castle.

(http://www.kelburngardenparty.com)

48. Indulge in Oysters on the Isle of Mull

If you are a fan of seafood, you'll know that the best seafood has to be eaten fresh, and it doesn't get much fresher than the sea treats found on the Isle of Mull, where fishing is one of the main industries of the island, which is surrounded by nutrient rich waters. The Isle of Mull is particularly famed for its incredible oysters. You can't go wrong sampling them at any restaurant or pub on the island, but we particularly like Am Birlinn, which specialises in local seafood.

(Dervaig, Tobermory, Isle of Mull; www.ambirlinn.com)

49. Visit Scotland's Oldest Public Museum

Culture vultures will not fail to be entertained and impressed on a trip to Scotland, and the oldest museum in the country, the Hunterian Museum & Gallery, also happens to be one of the best. Inside you can find artworks, ancient artefacts, a zoological collection, and lots more besides. We particularly like the exhibits and artefacts pertaining to Roman Scotland.

(University of Glasgow, University Ave, Glasgow; www.gla.ac.uk/hunterian)

50. Take in a Show at the Glasgow Royal Concert Hall

When you are in Glasgow and you want a night of culture, you can't do much better than to check out the almost unfailingly impressive programme of the Glasgow Royal Concert Hall. Now, we can't pretend that this is a grand auditorium that extends back for centuries as it only opened in 1990, but the folk there sure do know how to put on a show, particularly when it comes to classical music. If the Royal Scottish National Orchestra have something planned, book tickets without hesitation.

(Buchanan Galleries, 2 Sauchiehall St, Glasgow; www.glasgowconcerthalls.com/glasgow-royal-concert-hall)

51. Find Some Treasures at Out of the Blue Flea Market

As you walk through the streets of Edinburgh, you will find countless souvenir shops. But instead of taking back a tacky branded mug or tea-towel with you, wouldn't you prefer to take something home with you that's really special? Out of the Blue Flea Market is exactly the destination for that. It takes place every month, and you'll be able to find ornaments, paintings, prints, jewellery, vintage clothing, and more besides.

(www.outoftheblue.org.uk/out-of-the-blue-flea-market)

52. Explore Underwater Life at St Kilda

You might think that you have to travel to exotic destinations like Barbados or the Philippines in order to have an incredible diving experience in the ocean, but this is far from the case, and St Kilda in Scotland has earned its reputation as the holy grail of diving in the UK. As well as being able to dive in tunnels and caves, you'll see lots of spectacular sea life such as jellyfish, lobsters, and pollacks.

53. Eat Traditional Scottish Fare at Ubiquitous Chip

Glasgow is a city full of incredible restaurants, and if you're limited on time, it can be hard to know where you should go to have a meal that really impresses. Well, if it's Scottish fare that you're after, you can find it at its best at the Ubiquitous Chip. This is Scottish food using traditional ingredients, but with a twist. Instead of regular haggis, you'll find it made with venison, and the flaky Orkney Salmon comes served with cubes of horseradish jelly.

(12 Ashton Ln, Glasgow; www.ubiquitouschip.co.uk)

54. Be Wowed by Glasgow Cathedral

There is no shortage of historic architecture around Scotland, and one of the most impressive structures in the country has to be Glasgow Cathedral. The cathedral dates all the way back to the 12th century, and the patron saint of the city, Saint Mungo, is buried in the crypt. If you have the chance to watch an organ recital or choral performance in this incredible space, grab it with both hands.

(Castle St, Glasgow; www.glasgowcathedral.org)

55. Sip on Craft Beers at The Hanging Bat

Scotland is most definitely a great country for beer lovers, and if you want to taste the breadth and quality of craft beers in the country, we highly recommend swinging by The Hanging Bat in Edinburgh. Dark beers are definitely the specialty here, and you are given schooners of beer instead of pints, so you can really appreciate the taste of a few without being obliterated. And if you're hungry, they serve killer ribs and hot dogs.

(133 Lothian Rd, Edinburgh; http://thehangingbat.com)

56. Get Fired Up at Up Helly Aa

Up Helly Aa is the general name for any of the fire festivals that take place in the wintertime in Scotland to mark the end of the Yule season. While you'll be able to find a few of these celebrations at the end of January, the most famous takes place annually in Lerwick in the Shetlands. You'll find fire lit torches being paraded on the street with thousands of people looking on, and this then extends into an all-night party. *(www.uphellyaa.org)*

57. Try Your Hand at Skiing in Cairnwell

While it's true that many people go to Europe in the wintertime to enjoy skiing, you probably think of Switzerland or France as the primary skiing destinations. While these are great locations to hit the slopes, do not discount bonny Scotland. In Cairnwell, you'll actually find the largest ski centre in Scotland, where you can take lessons no matter your experience.

58. Discover Scotland's Nautical Culture at the Aberdeen Maritime Museum

Scotland is a country that is surrounded by water, and that means that it has an incredible maritime history. The best place to learn all about the Scottish people's connection to the North Sea is at the Aberdeen Maritime Museum. The museum has a very impressive collection, and you'll find exhibitions and artefacts related to shipbuilding, fishing, the oil industry, and sailing ships.

(Shiprow, Aberdeen; www.aagm.co.uk/Visit/AberdeenMaritimeMuseum/amm-overview.aspx)

59. Fill Your Stomach at the Loch Lomond Food & Drink Festival

One of the best things about visiting a new country is undoubtedly taking the opportunity to fill your stomach with as many treats as you can, and if you want to sample lots of new foods in one place, there is nothing better than the Loch Lomond Food & Drink Festival. It takes place each year at the beginning of September, and it attracts 30,000 visitors, making it one of the largest food events in the UK. You can watch cookery demos, eat restaurant plates, and take home lots of treats with you.

(www.lochlomondfoodanddrinkfestival.co.uk)

60. Taste Some Gin With Glasgow Gin Club

The people of Scotland do like to indulge with an occasional tipple, but if whisky isn't up your street, you might prefer the floral notes of gin. If so, you need to know about the Glasgow Gin Club, which pretty much does what it says on the tin. It's a group of people who are passionate about gin, and they get together to taste it. They regular hold tasting events, which are the perfect way to taste lots of lovely gin, and also to meet new people on your travels.

(https://theglasgowginclub.com)

61. Have a Water Skiing Adventure on Loch Ken

Fancy yourself as something of a daredevil? Well, Scotland is not just a country with old castles and picturesque landscapes – there are plenty of opportunities to raise your adrenaline too. Loch Ken is a beautiful lake in Scotland that has established itself as a premiere destination for watersports like sailing, windsurfing, and canoeing. There is even a water ski school on the lake so you can pick up a hair raising new skill.

62. Indulge a Sweet Tooth at the Perth Festival of Chocolate

Are you the kind of person who doesn't think a meal is complete until you've had dessert? If so, you'll be in sugar heaven at the Perth Festival of Chocolate, which takes place at the end of November each year. Throughout one long weekend, you can find market stalls that sell everything you could possibly imagine related to chocolate. There will be hot chocolate, chocolate cookies, chocolate cakes, artisanal chocolate bars, and lots more cocoa based goodness besides. *(www.perthfestivalofchocolate.co.uk)*

63. Raise Your Adrenaline at M&D's

If you are something of a thrill seeker, you might want to take a day off from sightseeing and museums, and spend a fun filled day at M&D's, which is the most popular amusement park in Scotland. The park contains two incredible rollercoasters, lots of fairground rides, and water rides to boot. If you are travelling with kids who get bored easily, this is where you can keep them happily entertained.

64. Enjoy the Spirit of the Highland Games

The Highland Games are a really big deal in Scotland, and the most popular of them all is the Cowal Highland Gathering, which takes place over the last weekend of August every year in the town of Dunoon. Witnessing these games is a real part of Scottish history because the Cowal Games were first held in 1894. Now the games attract 3500 competitors and 30,000 visitors every year. As well as sporting events, it's a great place for traditional music, dancing, and lots of merriment.
(Strathclyde Country Park, Bellshill, Motherwell; https://scotlandsthemepark.com)

65. Eat Tonnes of Seafood at Arbroath Seafest

Without a shadow of a doubt, Scotland is one of the best country's in the world for fans of seafood, and if you really can't get enough of trout, pike, crab, oysters, mussels, and the like, make your way to Arbroath Seafest, which takes place in mid-August each year, and attracts an impressive crowd of 30,000 people. The star of the show is always the Arbroath Smokie, a local smoked haddock that the local people are fiercely proud of.
(www.arbroathseafest.co.uk)

66. Find Peace in a Zen Garden in Glasgow

When you think of countries to visit for a spot of Zen, you'd probably think of somewhere in the Far East, but if you are in Scotland and in need of some focused tranquillity, you will also find a Zen garden in the heart of Glasgow. In fact, the garden, which you can find at the St Mungo Museum of Religious Life and Art, was the first Zen garden in the UK. It's a wonderful place to relax and just be.

(2 Castle St, Glasgow)

67. Celebrate Burns' Night Like a Local

The Scots love to party, and one of the most festive nights on the Scottish calendar is Burns' Night. On Burns' Night, the Scottish population celebrates the writings of beloved Scottish poet, Robert Burns. It lands on January 25th each year, the poet's birthday, and a Haggis dinner lies at the heart of the celebration. As the haggis is brought to the table, Burns' poem, Address to a Haggis, is recited to the table of guests, who then tuck in and wash their haggis down with copious amounts of Scottish whisky.

68. Enjoy a Decadent Meal at Braidwoods

The culinary scene in Scotland is certainly not limited to the main cities of Edinburgh and Glasgow, and this is something that you will discover if you make it to Braidwoods, a Michelin star restaurant set within a cottage in a small town called Dalry in Ayrshire. The food served up is certainly Scottish but always with an innovative twist. If the hand dived scallops are on the menu, order them without a second of hesitation.

(Dalry, Ayrshire; www.braidwoods.co.uk)

69. Find Something Special at Glasgow Art Fair

Once you have fallen in love with Scotland, you will no doubt want to take something home with you that will always remind you of the country. Take our advice and bypass the tacky tourist shops. Instead, head to Glasgow Art Fair, which is held in April each year, and is committed to supporting local talent and showcasing art that is also affordable for buyers.

(www.gcaf.co.uk)

70. Tuck Into Some Shetland Bannocks

Whenever you travel to a new place, part of the experience is trying the local food. You've no doubt heard of haggis before, but how about Shetland Bannocks? Bannocks are a speciality of Shetland, and they are basically a type of quickbread cooked in a round and then served up in wedges. The bannocks from Shetland are made with an ancient type of barley, and they are extremely filling and warming on a Scottish winter's day.

71. Rock Out at T in the Park

If there is one Scottish summer festival that you have already heard of, it is probably T in the Park. This is an outdoor music festival that is hosted every year in July, and has been running since 1994. Over a quarter of a million people make it to the festival each year, making it one of the most popular summer gatherings in Europe. In previous years, music acts such as Calvin Harris, Radiohead, The Human League, and Kasabian have performed.

(www.tinthepark.com)

72. Try a Traditional Scottish Dessert

Scottish food will warm you from the inside out, and honestly, that is something totally necessary with the cold weather that the country experiences. And when it comes to desserts, it is absolutely no different. Perhaps the most filling and warming of the lot is a clootie dumpling. This is a heavy suet pudding that is made with lots of dried fruit, black treacle, and warming spices, and is then steamed and served with cream or custard. Perfect for a chilly evening.

73. Have the Best NYE Ever at Hogmanay

The Scots sure do know how to throw a great party, and that's a good of a reason as any to tie your trip into the New Year's Eve celebrations. Hogmanay is very simply the local word for the last day of the year, but it has become synonymous with a party unlike any other. Experience Hogmanay in Scotland and you might see burning fireballs being thrown into the river, you'll be joining in with a raucous rendition of Auld Lang Syne whether you like it or not, and you'll be chugging back plenty of great whisky. *(www.edinburghshogmanay.com)*

74. Tour the Orkney Brewery

Beer is big business in Scotland, but if you want to extend your love of beer beyond sitting in the pub, we highly recommend making a trip to the island of Orkney and the Orkney Brewery. This brewery has a string of awards to its name, and it supplies customers all over the world, from Asia to the USA. On a tour, you can learn about the history of the brewery, the ins and outs of the production process, and, of course, you can sip on plenty of the good stuff.

(www.orkneybrewery.co.uk)

75. Enjoy Music at the Dundee Blues Bonanza

While Scotland is definitely not the place where blues music originated, if you are a fan of the smooth sounds of the blues, you'll love the Dundee Blues Bonanza, which takes place every year in July in the city of Dundee. Blues bands and musicians are invited from all over the UK to play their music in public spaces in the city. For one weekend, the city's population goes blues crazy. Will you be one of them?

(www.dundeebluesbonanza.co.uk)

76. Climb Britain's Highest Peak, Ben Nevis

If you are the kind of person who likes to get active on holiday instead of walking around museums, you might just have the most challenging outdoor adventure of your life in Scotland. Ben Nevis, the highest mountain in the UK standing tall at 1346 metres, is just waiting to be climbed. If you are not a very experienced walker, there is a tourist path that can take you to the peak in less than five hours. It will be a slog, but the view will be more than enough of a reward.

77. Sip on 100 Teas at Tchai-Ovna

When exploring the cities of Scotland, Glasgow is too often neglected in favour of its big bro, Edinburgh, but there are so many awesome eating and drinking haunts in Glasgow that it's a pleasure to explore the culinary delights of the city. Tchai-Ovna is one such place. This quaint tea-house serves up 100 types of tea, and the stuff really know their stuff. There's also vegetarian food, and live gigs with a local crowd around five nights a week.

(42 Otago Ln, Glasgow; www.tchaiovna.com)

78. Down a Pint in Scotland's Remotest Pub

There is no shortage of fantastic pubs to enjoy a refreshing pint of ale in Scotland, but the most special of them all might be The Old Forge, which is listed in the Guinness Book of Records as the remotest pub in mainland Britain. In fact, if you want to reach this treasure, you'll have to hike for eighteen miles to get there. Once you smell the venison cooking in the kitchen, you will realise that the hike is totally worth it.

(Inverie, Knoydart, Mallaig; www.theoldforge.co.uk)

79. Enjoy the Fine White Sand of Eigg

If you are the kind of traveller who likes to get away from it all and just immerse yourself in natural beauty, it's imperative that you make at least a couple of trips away from the mainland. The Isle of Eigg is a veritable paradise, and the highlight has to be a stretch of beach on the north west side of the island called Laig Bay. From the look of the white sand, you might wonder whether you are really in Scotland. Alas, the nip in the air will remind you sooner rather than later.

80. Embrace Your Inner Hippie at The Wickerman Festival

The annual Wickerman Festival, which takes place every July in the beautiful countryside is the music festival for you if you are really into alternative music. You'll find world music, punk, ska, lo-fi, indie, and lots more exciting music to discover. The festival definitely attracts a hippie contingent, which is no bad thing, so all you have to do is buy your ticket and feel the positive vibes. Acts that have played in the past include Primal Scream, The Charlatans, and Hot Chip.

81. See Ospreys Up Close at Loch Garten

Ospreys are some of the most beautiful birds that you are ever likely to see. These fish eating birds of prey used to be commonplace in Britain, but due to careless behaviour towards them, they could no longer be found in Britain by the early 20th century. Fortunately, thanks to incredible conservation work, some ospreys have been attracted back to Scotland, and Loch Garten is the place to be if you want to see these magnificent birds up close.

82. Get Outdoorsy at the Wild Spring Festival

There are endless opportunities to get back to nature in Scotland, and you can explore the incredible breadth of wildlife in the country at the Wild Spring Festival, which is hosted each year in March and April each year, in south-west Scotland. The festival allows you to really appreciate nature in a different way. There will be conservation days, Easter Egg hunts in nature, hikes through the countryside, and lots more outdoorsy goodness besides.

(www.wildspringfestival.com)

83. Explore the Ruins of Dryburgh Abbey

Scotland has an incredible history, and it's possible to explore some of this history for yourself in the ruin sites located around the country. One of our favourites is the remarkably well preserved ruins of Dryburgh Abbey, a medieval abbey that dates all the way back to the 12th century, and is set against the picturesque River Tweed. You can also find the burial place of Sir Walter Scott on site.

84. Eat a Decadent Gelato at Affogato

Okay, Scotland isn't exactly known as a paradise of summer sunshine, but if you do happen to be in Edinburgh during its short summer and you need something delicious to cool you down, head straight for Affogato, which serves up the very best ice cream in the city. The rose and lychee flavour is something very special if you fancy something out of the ordinary. And if it's a cold day, they also serve fresh waffles and coffee – yum!

(36 Queensferry St, Edinburgh; http://affogatogelato.co.uk)

85. Party Around the Lake at Groove Loch Ness

Loch Ness has to be one of the most iconic locations on the face of the planet. But while it is most well known for being the home of the mythical Loch Ness monster, Nessie, it's also a place where, once a year, people love to drink, dance, and have one hell of a party. Groove Loch Ness is a relatively new festival, hosted under the stars every August, and that has attracted talent such as Groove Armada and Duke Dumont.

(www.groovefestival.co.uk)

86. Stay Overnight in a Lighthouse

When you travel around a country, you probably stay in guesthouses, hotels, and hostels, or maybe you'll try a spot of Couchsurfing. But if you fancy staying somewhere a little more special than the average, etch a trip to the Rua Reidh Lighthouse, which stands at the entrance of Loch Ewe, into your travel diary. This is a functional lighthouse with rooms for guests. From your window, you have the opportunity to spot dolphins, sea eagles, otters, and even whales.

(Melvaig, Gairloch; https://stayatalighthouse.co.uk)

87. Have a Hearty Slice of Dundee Cake

In true British tradition, Scots do like to have a slice of cake and a cup of tea, and perhaps the most popular cake in all of the country is Dundee Cake. The cake has roots that extend back for more than 350 years, and, of course, the best place to tuck into a slice is in the city of Dundee. This cake is not for the faint hearted. It is dense and full of fruit, including currants and sultanas, and you'll find a sprinkling of almonds over the top.

88. Look at Puffins on Handa Island

If it's wildlife that really gets you excited, a trip to Handa Island off the west coast of the country is an absolute must visit. On the island, you can find red deer, razorbills, guillemots, otters, seals, dolphins, and even whales. But there's one animal that people take the Handa Ferry especially for, and that's the puffin. Seeing puffins climbing over the cliff faces in their natural habitat is something truly magical and once in a lifetime.

(www.handa-ferry.com)

89. Buy Some Beautiful Shetland Knitwear

If you spend any time in the Scottish countryside on your trip, you will immediately recognise the amount of cattle and farm animals that roam the land. Some of this is for food, but the beautiful sheep in the Shetland area are well known for their fluffy coat of fur that creates some of the softest wool on the planet. When it Shetland, be sure to pop into the farm shops and small boutiques to purchase the one of a kind knitwear items from the area.

90. Take a Sled-Dog Ride Through the Cairngorms

Although Scotland is a wonderful country to visit at any time of the year, we think that it's particularly beautiful in the winter. And if you love snow and winter sports, this is definitely the time to make your trip. Something really unique that you can do up in the snowy Cairngorm Mountains is take a sled-dog ride. If you're travelling with kids, it's something that they will particularly love, and it makes a great festive experience in the Christmas period.

91. Eat at Michelin Star Restaurant, Number One

When going on holiday, everybody has to stick to some kind of budget, but it's still important to indulge now and again, and what better way to get a little decadent than at a Michelin star restaurant? Our pick would have to be Number One in Edinburgh, a restaurant that serves up Scottish fine dining at its very best. If you can splurge, do go for the tasting menu so that you can sample a little bit of all the incredible deliciousness.

(Balmoral Hotel, 1 Princes St, Edinburgh; www.roccofortehotels.com/hotels-and-resorts/the-balmoral-hotel/restaurants-and-bars/number-one)

92. Get Artsy With the LeithLate Festival

Leith can be thought of as the trendy neighbourhood of Edinburgh, and if you want to feel the creativity of Scotland, this is the place to do so. Each year, the neighbourhood hosts its own LeithLate Festival, which involves many exciting creative projects. You could go on a mural tour of the city, you could witness a panel discussion by local artists, and you can purchase lots of great art work for your own home.

(www.leithlate.co.uk)

93. Sip on Cocktails at Kelvingrove Café

After a long day of sightseeing, what more could you want than to sip on an indulgent cocktail or two? In Glasgow, the best place to go for a cocktail is the Kelvingrove Café, a beautiful brasserie bar with wood panelling and leather banquettes that will make you feel immersed in luxury immediately. And then the cocktails will take you all the way. Our favourite might be the East Coast Trilogy, which has the very Scottish flavours of whisky and tea.

(1161 Argyle Street, Glasgow; www.kelvingrovecafe.com)

94. Scale to the Top of the Scott Monument

Sir Walter Scott is one of the most important writers in the history of literature, and the Scott Monument is a gothic structure that was created in memory of the man himself. It is, in fact, the tallest monument to a writer anywhere in the world, and if you are feeling daring, you can actually trek up to the top of it. The climb up 287 steps can be arduous to say the least, but the view of Edinburgh from the top is well worth the slog.

(E. Princes St Gardens, Edinburgh)

95. Discover Prehistoric Scotland

If you make it to the Shetland Islands, as you absolutely should, you can find a prehistoric site whose history extends back to 2700BC. Jarlshof is really spectacular because there is evidence of 4000 years of history at this one site. You will be able to see Iron Age wheelhouses, Norse long houses, a medieval farmstead, and a rich collection of ancient artefacts in the visitor's centre.

(www.shetland-heritage.co.uk/jarlshof)

96. Wave a Rainbow Flag at Pride Scotia

The Scottish have earned the reputation of being warm, friendly, and open-minded people, and that is reflected in the progressive attitude to LGBT rights in the country. Pride Scotia is the principle gay pride event in the country, and there are pride events in both Edinburgh and Glasgow. The pinnacle of the celebrations is also a colourful parade through the streets of the cities with music pumping, people dancing, and lots of positive vibes.

(58/2 Broughton St, Edinburgh; http://prideedinburgh.org.uk)

97. Go Meat Free at the Edinburgh Vegan Festival

Travelling as a vegetarian can be difficult, and as a vegan even more so. Fortunately, you can find veggie friendly dishes in almost all restaurants across the country, but if you want to bask in vegan bliss, you should time your trip to coincide with the Edinburgh Vegan Festival, which takes place towards the end of August each year. Highlights include talks to help you out with the vegan lifestyle you want to have, and, of course, all the food that will be on offer.

98. Watch a Concert at Usher Hall

If you like a reason to get all dressed up of an evening time, you should know about Usher Concert Hall, which has to be the most spectacular of all the music venues in the city. It has been drawing in the crowds every night for more than a century, and it's a particularly great space to know about if you have an interest in classical music. The venue is the home of the Royal National Scottish Orchestra, and the Scottish Chamber Orchestra often plays there as well.
(Lothian Rd, Edinburgh; www.usherhall.co.uk)

99. Explore a Medieval Fortress on a Cliff Face

Scotland is a country full of ruins and historical buildings, and one of the most special of them all is certainly Dunnottar Castle. This ruined medieval fortress is located on the edge of a headland, and the view out on to the ocean combined with the ruins is something very special. The surviving buildings are from the 15th and the 16th centuries.
(www.dunnottarcastle.co.uk)

100. Catch a Movie at Glasgow Film Theatre

Let's face it, the weather in Scotland isn't always exactly how you would want it to be. But fear not because there are plenty of rainy day activities to enjoy on a trip to Scotland, and in

Glasgow, the best might just be the Glasgow Film Theatre. Yes, this is a cinema, but it's not just a run of the mill place that shows Hollywood blockbusters. Glasgow Film Theatre is an independent cinema located in a listed building where you can watch documentaries, international picks, and the old classics.

(12 Rose St, Glasgow; http://glasgowfilm.org)

101. Enjoy a Drink With a View in Glasgow

Glasgow is a very charming city, but it's impossible to appreciate the full beauty of the city when you are simply walking around the streets, so why not explore one of the city's rooftop bars? Well, actually there is only one, and it is at The Carlton George hotel. The bar is located on the 7th floor so you have a lovely view over the city, and their food and drink is pretty great too. Their afternoon tea is a little over a tenner and offers incredible value that cannot be beaten.

(44 W George St, Glasgow; www.carlton.nl/en/hotel-george-glasgow)

Before You Go…

Hey you! Thanks so much for reading **101 Coolest Things to Do in Scotland.** We really hope that this helps to make your time in Scotland the most fun and memorable trip that it can be.

Keep your eyes peeled on www.101coolestthings.com and have a wonderful trip!

Team 101 Coolest Things

Made in the USA
San Bernardino, CA
05 March 2017